[A Maths]

JOURNEY

<= ~ ± ÷ ⟩around⟨

Pl net

Earth

CONTENTS

go figure

As the leader of an ecological expedition, your job is to use your mathematical knowledge to explore different regions of the world that are affected by natural events, climate change or human beings.

Learn about tallies, Roman numerals, volume, decimals and other mathematical principles and then use them to solve puzzles that will guide you on your mission around the globe!

Answers to the Go Figure! challenges can be found on page 28.

Words in *italics* appear in the glossary on page 30.

You might find some of the questions in this book are too hard to do without the help of a calculator.
Ask your teacher about when and how to use a calculator.

WHAT EQUIPMENT DO YOU NEED?

Pen or pencil

Notepad

Ruler

AROUND THE WORLD

Your first mission takes you to China, where you are looking at how people have moved around over long periods of time.

LEARN ABOUT IT
WORKING WITH LARGE NUMBERS

It is often useful to be able to see which is the larger of two or more numbers. We use the symbols >, < or = to show how numbers compare.

< means the first number is smaller than the second. | **5 + 1 < 8**

> means the first number is larger than the second. | **6 − 2 > 1**

= means the two numbers are equal (the same). | **3 + 2 = 5**

Compare these changing *population* figures for two Chinese towns: Key: = 100 people

YEAR	TOWN A	TOWN B	TOTAL
1900			
1950			
2000			

In 1900, Town A had 900 people and Town B had 700: **900 > 700**
In 1950, Town A had 800 people and Town B had 800: **800 = 800**
In 1950, the total population was 1,600 and in 2000 it was 1,900: **1,600 < 1,900**

⟩GO FIGURE!

You are studying a town in China which has kept records of its population for a long time. You have records of people who lived there permanently, and the "floating" population of people who drifted in and out.

Year	Permanent population	Floating population
2008	234,117	451
1721	268,712	2,312
1919	242,419	740
1602	251,991	5,708
1871	239,022	4,219

1. Was the total population of the town larger in 1871 or 2008?

2. **When was the earliest data recorded?**

3. Put the correct signs <, > or = between these pairs of numbers:

   242,419 • 234,117
   234,117 • 239,022
   251,991 • 268,712

4. **Write out in words the permanent population in 1602.**

5. When did most people live in the town, including floating and permanent populations?

6. **In your notepad, list the records in order of total population, starting with the lowest first.**

ERUPTING GEYSERS

Your next mission takes you to Iceland to record the eruptions of a geyser. This is a natural hot spring that regularly shoots huge jets of boiling water into the air.

LEARN ABOUT IT
TALLIES AND FREQUENCY TABLES

Many types of data are recorded by counting or tallying. Keeping a *tally* is easier than counting as you make a mark for each item or event you see.

$\mathbf{|} = 1$ $\mathbf{||||} = 4$ $\cancel{||||} = 5$

Draw four lines for the first four items, then draw a line through that group for the fifth. This makes it easy to count up later:

$\cancel{||||}\ \cancel{||||}\ |||$

This tally shows (2 x 5) + 3 = 13

If you record tallies in a frequency *table*, you can write the number in the last column. For example, this table shows a tally of the number of days two team members have spent on your Icelandic expedition:

	Days spent on expedition	Frequency
Alice	$\cancel{||||}\ \cancel{||||}\ \cancel{||||}\ |$	16
Gabriel	$\cancel{||||}\ \cancel{||||}\ \cancel{||||}\ \cancel{||||}\ ||$	22

This first table shows the number of eruptions you recorded on each day this week:

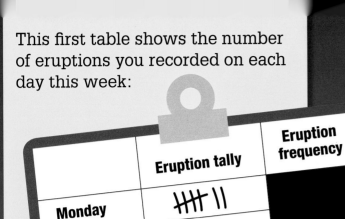

	Eruption tally	Eruption frequency
Monday	ǁǁǁ ǁǁ	
Tuesday	ǁǁǁǁ	
Wednesday	ǁǁǁǁ	
Thursday	ǁǁǁ	
Friday	ǁǁǁǁ	

This table shows the number of days that had a particular number of eruptions:

Number of days	Number of eruptions per day
2	6
3	4
4	3
5	2

1. In the first table, how many days had four eruptions?

2. **Copy out the first table in your notepad and fill in the last column with the number of eruptions on each day?**

3. Looking at the second table, how many days did your team take records for?

4. **How many eruptions were recorded in the second table?**

5. If you were going to draw a chart of your results, would it be better to make a *bar chart*, a *pie chart* or a line chart? Why?

FOSSIL HUNTING

You have travelled to Mongolia where dinosaur fossils have been found. You have been tasked to buy fossils for a museum back home.

LEARN ABOUT IT
WORKING WITH MONEY

Working with money is the same as working with any other *decimal* numbers.

Sometimes, you might have to work to a budget. This means there is a limited amount of money to spend. Aside from the fossils, you have £20 to spend on supplies for your fossil trip. You have found some things you would like to buy:

If you add up all the numbers, these items come to £24.32, so you cannot afford all of them. You need to reduce your bill by £4.32. You could put back the first aid box and the tools, or just the water.

If you paid with a £20 note for the food and the water, you would get:

£20 – (£10.99 + £7.95) = £1.06 change

FOSSIL HUNTERS SUPPLIES RECEIPT

FIRST AID BOX £2.40

FOOD.............................£10.99

WATER.............................£7.95

TOOLS.............................£2.98

TOTAL **£24.32**

This is the price list for the different fossils:

PRICE LIST

FOSSIL 1 £105.39

FOSSIL 2 £97.12

FOSSIL 3 £73.40

FOSSIL 4 £34.75

1. What is the difference in price between fossil number 1 and fossil number 2?

2. **Which fossil is the cheapest?**

3. You have £200. What is the largest number of fossils you can buy?

4. **You decide to buy fossils 2 and 4. What are the prices of each, rounded to the nearest £10?**

5. You pay for fossils 2 and 4 with seven £20 notes. How much change do you get?

TAKING FOSSILS HOME

You have bought some fossils and now you need to work out how much space they will take up on the flight home and how many boxes you will need to pack them.

LEARN ABOUT IT

CUBIC UNITS AND VOLUME

The *volume* of a three-dimensional object is the amount of space it takes up. Volume is measured in cubic units, such as cubic metres (m^3), or cubic centimetres (cm^3).

If you imagine a shape made up of *cubes* with sides of one metre, you could work out the volume by counting the cubes.

The volume of each cube is worked out by multiplying the base x depth x height:

$$1 \times 1 \times 1 = 1 \ m^3$$

This shape is made up of six cubes. It has two rows of three cubes:

$$2 \times 3 = 6 \text{ cubic units}$$
$$\text{Total volume} = 6 \ m^3$$

The volume of this shape is three cubic units.

You can rearrange the cubes and the volume remains the same.

The volume of a shape is often used in other calculations. If each cube was a box that contained 12 fossils, you could work out the total number of fossils.

This shape contains 3 x 12 = 36 fossils.

⟩GO FIGURE!

All the fossils you have bought have been packed up into boxes and piled up ready to be sent home. The volume of each box is 1 m³.

Check List

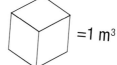

= 1 m³

Number of cubes?

Book transport

Transport cost (£2.12 per m³)

1. You need to book transport for the boxes. What is the total volume of the boxes?

2. **To transport the boxes costs £2.12 per m³. How much will it cost?**

3. What would the stack of boxes look like if you stood in front of the short edge and looked at it? Draw a picture of it in your notepad.

4. **Draw another arrangement of the boxes with the same volume.**

GEMSTONES IN POMPEII

You are visiting the ancient city of Pompeii, which was destroyed by a volcanic eruption of Mount Vesuvius in 79 CE. The records you discover there use *Roman numerals* instead of numbers.

LEARN ABOUT IT
ROMAN NUMERALS

The Romans did not use the number system we use. Instead, they used letters to represent numbers.

1	I
5	V
10	X
50	L
100	C
500	D
1,000	M

They combined letters to make numbers. Counting up to 3 is easy:

I, II, III

But they did not use more than three of the same letter in a row.

'4' is shown as '5 − 1': put the 'I' before the 'V' to show it is taken away:

4 = IV

Numbers over 5 use 'V' and 'I'. Put the letter for the largest number first:

VI (5 + 1 = 6), VII (5 + 2 = 7), VIII (5 + 3 = 8)

Each time you get to three of the same letter in a row, it is time to use the 'minus 1' method.

So '9' is '10 − 1', shown as 'IX':

9 = IX (10 − 1 = 9)

12

Bigger numbers can get quite long. For example:

39 = XXXIX

XXX (for 30) + IX (10 – 1 = 9)

388 = CCCLXXXVIII

CCC (3 x 100) + L (50) + XXX (3 x 10) + V (5) + III (3 x 1)

These numbers show the pattern:

1, 2, 3	I, II, III	40	XL (= 50 – 10)
4	IV	50	L
5	V	60, 70, 80	LX, LXX, LXXX
6, 7, 8	VI, VII, VIII	90	XC (= 100 – 10)
9, 10	IX, X	99	XCIX (= 100 – 10 + 10 – 1)
11, 12, 13	XI, XII, XIII	100	C
14, 15	XIV, XV	201	CCI
19, 20	XIX, XX	437	CDXXXVII
30	XXX	500	D

⟩GO FIGURE!

You see a slate with the accounts of a Roman gem trader. The figures show how many gems the trader sold and how many he stocked.

ITEM	NUMBER STOCKED	NUMBER SOLD
DIAMONDS	XL	XXIX
EMERALDS	XCIV	
RUBIES	XXXVI	XXXVI
PEARLS	CCLV	

1. How many pearls did the gem trader stock?

2. **How many diamonds were unsold?**

3. All the rubies sold, so the gem trader made a note to buy twice as many on his next sales trip. What did he write down?

4. **The gem trader did not fill in the column for emeralds that had** sold, but 15 were found in the ruins of the shop. How many had he sold? How would you write that in Roman numerals?

VOLCANIC THREAT

You have journeyed to Indonesia to study an active volcano. You need to take measurements and create a map of the region to *estimate* the damage that a volcanic eruption might cause.

LEARN ABOUT IT
SCALE DRAWING AND MULTIPLYING NUMBERS WITH ZEROS

14

A *scale* drawing or map is an accurate image of a scene that has been drawn smaller or larger than real life.

Maps are usually drawn to scale. You can use a ruler to measure a distance on scale maps and know exactly how far you have to travel. Scale drawings show the scale that has been used. To work out the real size or distance, multiply by the scale.

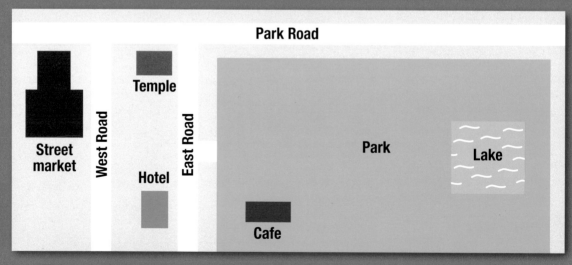

This map is at a scale of 1:10,000, Use your ruler to measure distances between objects on the map and then multiply by 10,000 to find out the real distance. For example, the lake is 2 cm wide, so in real life it is:

2 x 10,000 = 20,000 cm = 200 m

〉GO FIGURE!

This map shows where the volcano is. You want to help the local people work out whether they will be in danger if the volcano erupts. Places up to 50 km away from the volcano are in danger.

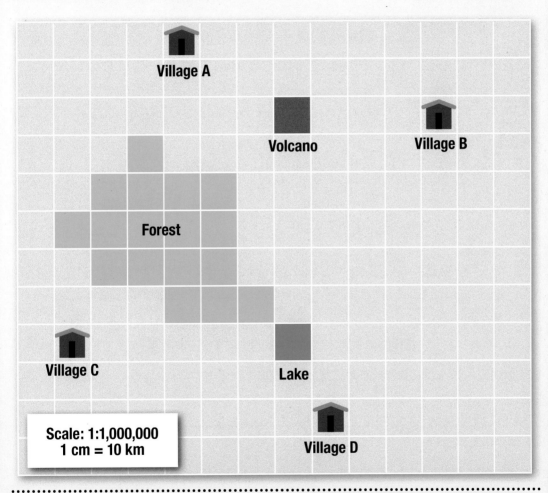

Village A

Volcano

Village B

Forest

Village C

Lake

Village D

Scale: 1:1,000,000
1 cm = 10 km

1. Which villages would be in danger if the volcano erupted?

2. How far is it from the volcano to the lake (to the nearest 10 km)?

3. The *area* of each square is 100 km². What area is covered by the forest?

4. If each 1 km² of forest contains 5,000 trees, how many trees are in each square of forest?

5. How many trees are in the whole forest?

MELTING MOUNTAIN ICE

You have ventured to the chilly Himalayan Mountains to see how global warming is affecting the rate at which the glaciers are melting.

LEARN ABOUT IT
DIVISION

16

***Division* helps you to work out shares or portions of numbers. You can think of division as taking one number away from another several times over.**

You can take 12 away from 48 four times, so $48 \div 12 = 4$:

$$48 - 12 = 36$$
$$36 - 12 = 24$$
$$24 - 12 = 12$$
$$12 - 12 = 0$$

Division is the opposite of multiplying.

$$48 \div 12 = 4 \text{ so } 4 \times 12 = 48$$

If the sum is harder, you need to break it down – for example, if you wanted to divide 2,520 by 7:

Write the numbers like this:

$$7\overline{)2520}$$

Try dividing the first digit by 7: $2 \div 7$ does not work.

Try with the first two digits:
$25 \div 7$
$7 \times 3 = 21$, so 7 will go into 25 three times.

$$7\overline{)2520} \\ 21 \\ 3$$

Put '3' above the sum and '21' underneath.

Show the subtraction to get the remainder: 25 − 21 = 4:

```
      3
  7 | 2520
      21
      ---
      4
```

Bring down the next digit, 2, and put it beside 4 to make 42:

```
      3
  7 | 2520
      21
      ---
      42
```

7 goes into 42 exactly 6 times with no remainder:

```
      36
  7 | 2520
      21
      ---
      42
      42
      ---
      0
```

Bring down the last digit, 0. 7 will not go into 0 at all, so write 0 above the line:

```
      360
  7 | 2520
      21
      ---
      42
      42
      ---
      00
```

And that is the answer: 360. You can check by doing the sum 7 x 360 = 2,520.

⟩GO FIGURE!

During your time on the glacier, you estimate that about 43,740 litres of water will flow from the glacier in total.

1 If this volume of water melts over nine days, how many litres will flow each day?

2 **You were given the wrong information. The volume of water melts over 90 days. How many litres of water flow each day?**

3 Sixty households share the water from the glacier. How much water will each household have per day?

4 **If the water flows too quickly, it floods the fields. To prevent this, it is divided between two channels. How much water flows through each channel every day?**

5 If each channel was then used to water, or irrigate, three fields, how much water would each field receive per day?

FEELING COLDER

You have gone to Greenland to investigate the climate and, in particular, the temperature. Greenland is a very cold place, where the temperature regularly falls below 0°C.

LEARN ABOUT IT

POSITIVE AND NEGATIVE NUMBERS

***Negative numbers* are numbers that are less than zero. *Positive numbers* are numbers that are greater than zero.**

18

On a *number line*, the negative numbers are to the left of zero and the positive numbers are to the right of zero:

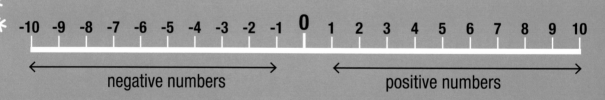

-10 -9 -8 -7 -6 -5 -4 -3 -2 -1 **0** 1 2 3 4 5 6 7 8 9 10

negative numbers   positive numbers

Some subtraction sums give an answer less than zero – a negative answer. If you take away 5 from 3, for example, the answer is -2. This is easy to see using a number line:

-10 -9 -8 -7 -6 -5 -4 -3 -2 -1 **0** 1 2 3 4 5 6 7 8 9 10

$$3 - 5 = -2$$

Numbers get smaller as you move to the left of the number line –
so -7 is a smaller number than -3. Numbers get larger as you
move to the right of the number line.

-10 -9 -8 -7 -6 -5 -4 -3 -2 -1 **0** 1 2 3 4 5 6 7 8 9 10

← →

range -10 to 10

The range of this number line is 20, going from -10 to 10.

〉GO FIGURE!

Because the temperature in Greenland gets very low, the
thermometer you are using shows negative numbers.

-20 -19 -18 -17 -16 -15 -14 -13 -12 -11 -10 -9 -8 -7 -6 -5 -4 -3 -2 -1 0 1 2 3 4 5

1 The temperature now is 3°C. At night, it might go to -11°C. What is the difference in temperature?

2 Sometimes the temperature is less than -15°C. How many degrees below -15°C does the thermometer show?

3 Yesterday the temperature at different times of the day was: -8°C, -1°C, 4°C, -3°C. What was the highest temperature yesterday?

4 What was the lowest temperature yesterday?

5 What was the range of the temperatures recorded?

MONSOON TIME

You are in the Philippines during the rainy season called monsoon. Heavy rainfall is normal for this time of year.

LEARN ABOUT IT
PICTOGRAMS

A *pictogram* is a chart that uses small pictures or icons to show a number of items or a measurement. It is easy to compare values with a pictogram.

This pictogram uses pictures to show what the weather is like for each hour during a 24-hour period:

24-HOUR WEATHER FORECAST

1 am–8 am							
9 am–4 pm							
5 pm–12 am							

From this, you can see that there were six hours of sunshine, four hours of rain and a total of 14 hours of cloudy weather in total.

A pictogram is not a good way to show numbers exactly. If there were 40 minutes of sunshine, you might show $^2/_3$ of a Sun, but it would just look like more than half a Sun. When you draw your own pictograms, you need to choose carefully how to represent numbers. You need to show different things using different images, but too many could make the pictogram confusing.

〉GO FIGURE!

Scientists at the research station you visit have kept a record of rainfall over the past few weeks. They have created a pictogram for you.

	RAINFALL
Week 1	☁☁☁☁☁☁
Week 2	☁☁☁☁☁☁☁◖
Week 3	☁☁☁☁☁
Week 4	████████████

☁ = 1 cm rain

1. How many centimetres of rain fell in Week 2?

2. **What is the total rainfall for the first three weeks?**

3. Week 4 had 7.5 cm rain. In your notepad, draw the correct number of rainclouds for the last row.

4. **The daily rainfall during Week 5 was:**

Monday	1.3 cm	Friday	1.1 cm
Tuesday	0.8 cm	Saturday	0.9 cm
Wednesday	1.2 cm	Sunday	1.0 cm
Thursday	1.4 cm		

Draw a pictogram of your own to show these figures. Use one raincloud = 0.2 cm rain.

SNOWED IN!

You are in Antarctica, but the weather is bad and you cannot leave. Your team has found various graphs and plots showing the predicted conditions in the area.

There are lots of different types of graphs and charts. Some are more suitable for showing continuous data – figures taken from a constant stream of possible readings.

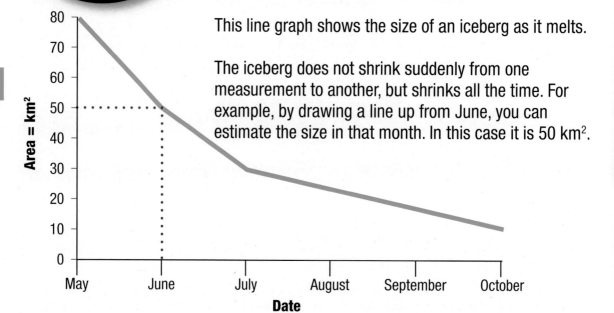

This line graph shows the size of an iceberg as it melts.

The iceberg does not shrink suddenly from one measurement to another, but shrinks all the time. For example, by drawing a line up from June, you can estimate the size in that month. In this case it is 50 km^2.

Other types of chart are more suitable for showing separate amounts. *Line plots*, bar charts and pie charts are good for this type of data. This line plot shows how many icebergs were seen over three months.

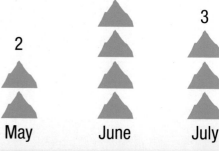

〉GO FIGURE!

Your team has found a temperature graph as well as a line plot showing the number of icebergs that will be seen in the area.

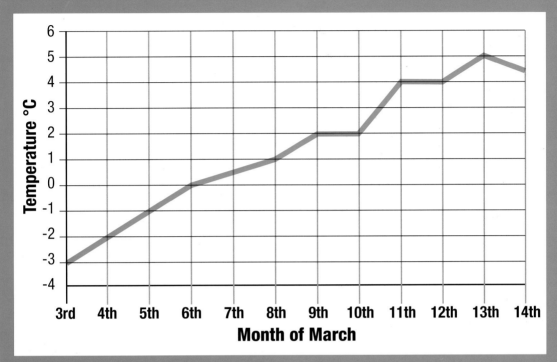

1. What will the temperature be on the 9th March?

2. **You can travel when the temperature reaches 4°C or more. When will this happen?**

3. What is the highest predicted temperature?

4. **When will you see the most icebergs?**

5. How many will you see from Monday to Thursday?

6. **On Friday you will see three icebergs. How many icebergs will that make for the entire week?**

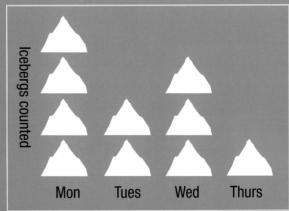

DEEP-SEA DIVING

You have taken a submarine to see how the coral is growing on a tropical reef near Sydney, Australia. In particular, you are recording the shapes the coral grows in.

LEARN ABOUT IT
PLANE AND SOLID SHAPES

Flat, or *plane shapes* are two-dimensional. The simplest plane shape is a *triangle*, which has three sides.

triangle

24

Shapes with four sides are quadrilaterals. Those with four *right angles* are squares or *rectangles*. A square has four sides of the same length. A quadrilateral without right angles can be a parallelogram, a trapezium or a rhombus.

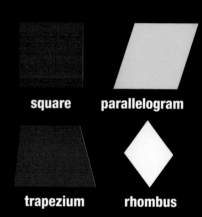

square   parallelogram

trapezium   rhombus

Here are some other shapes with more sides:

5 pentagon   6 hexagon   7 heptagon   8 octagon

A regular shape with a curved outline can be a circle or an ellipse.

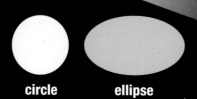

circle   ellipse

Solid shapes are three-dimensional. Here are some regular solid shapes.

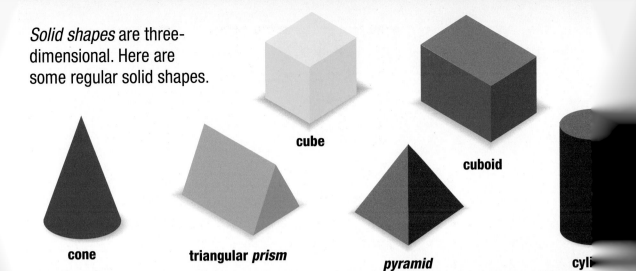

cube

cuboid

cone

triangular _prism_

pyramid

cyl...

⟩GO FIGURE!

From your submarine, you check the coral shapes in two regions, or zones, of the coral reef.

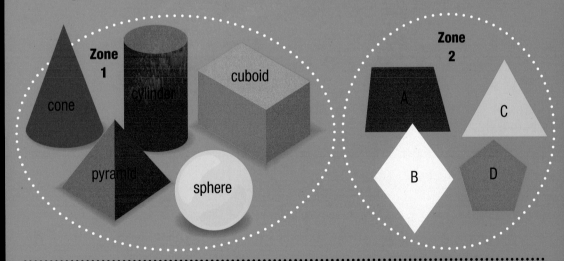

Zone 1

cone

cylinder

cuboid

pyramid

sphere

Zone 2

A

B

C

D

1 One piece of coral in Zone 1 has a round base and it gets narrower until it comes to a point at the top. Which shape could it be?

2 Another piece of coral has four sides, a top and a bottom that are all straight. Two sides are longer than the other two. What shape is it?

3 The coral in Zone 2 is growing in two-dimensional shapes – A, B, C and D. Which is a rhombus?

4 What is the total number of sides of the coral shapes found in Zone 2?

5 Which coral shape in Zone 2 has five sides?

GLOBAL TIME

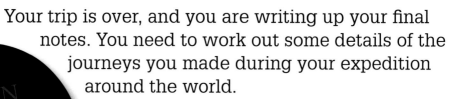

Your trip is over, and you are writing up your final notes. You need to work out some details of the journeys you made during your expedition around the world.

We can tell the time using an *analogue* clock or a *digital* clock.

A digital clock can work as a 12-hour clock or a 24-hour clock. A 12-hour clock shows numbers from 00:00 to 12:00 for both morning (am) and afternoon to evening (pm). A 24-hour clock numbers the hours from 00:00 to 24:00.

Analogue clock (12-hr)
3.40 pm

Digital clock (24-hr)
15:40

The world is divided into time zones.

New York
-5 hours

London

Athens +2 hours

-11 -10 -9 -8 -7 -6 -5 -4 -3 -2 -1 0 +1 +2 +3 +4 +5 +6 +7 +8 +9 +10 +11 +12

When it is 12:00 in London, it is -5 hours (earlier) in New York, so 07:00. In Athens, it is +2 hours (later), so 14:00.

For example, you leave Athens at 10 am and it takes 5 hours to get to London. To find out the time in London when you arrive, you need to take away 2 hours (the time difference) and then need to add 5 hours (the flight time).

LEAVE ATHENS		ARRIVE IN LONDON (+ 5 HOURS)	
Athens time	London time	**Athens time**	London time
10:00	08:00	**15:00**	13:00

⟩GO FIGURE!

You have plotted a map of the places you have visited, along with their time zones. Some countries choose their own time zones, and these might not be the same as other places in the region. For example, Iceland has the same time zone as London.

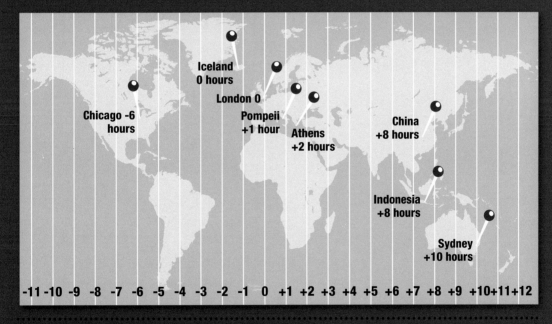

1. You arrived in Indonesia at 3 pm. What time was it in Pompeii?

2. You arrived in Sydney at 17:30 local time and phoned a friend in Chicago. What time was it in Chicago?

3. The distance from China to Iceland is nearly 8,000 km. If the plane flies at 800 km/h, how long will the flight last?

4. If your flight leaves China at 6 am, what is the time in Iceland when you arrive?

5. Your phone shows the time using the 24 hour clock — write down the local departure and arrival times for the China to Iceland flight.

GO FIGURE! ANSWERS

04-05 Around the world

1. 1871

2. 1602

3. 242,419 > 234,117
234,117 < 239,022
251,991 < 268,712

4. Two hundred and fifty-one thousand, nine hundred and ninety-one.

5. 1721

6.

Year	Total population
2008	234,568
1919	243,159
1871	243,241
1602	257,699
1721	271,024

06-07 Erupting geysers

1. Two days – Tuesday and Friday

2.

	Tally	Frequency
Monday	卌 ||	7
Tuesday	||||	4
Wednesday	卌	5
Thursday	|||	3
Friday	||||	4

3. 2 + 3 + 4 + 5 = 14 days

4. (2 x 6) + (3 x 4) + (4 x 3) + (5 x 2) =
12 + 12 + 12 + 10 = 46 eruptions

5. A bar chart would be best because it shows separate sets of data as different entries.

08-09 Fossil hunting

1. £105.39 – £97.12 = £8.27

2. Fossil 4

3. Two; the cheapest three all together cost £205.27

4. Fossil 2: £100; Fossil 4: £30

5. 7 x £20 = £140 to spend
£97.12 + £34.75 = £131.87
£140 – £131.87 = £8.13

10-11 Taking fossils home

1. 2 x 2 x 3 = 12 m^3

2. £2.12 x 12 = £25.44

3.

4. Here are some patterns you can arrange the boxes in, but there are lots of others:

12-13 Gemstones in Pompeii

1. 255

2. 40 – 29 = 11

3. 2 x 36 = 72, so he wrote LXXII

4. He had 94; 94 – 15 = 79, which is LXXIX

14-15 Volcanic threat

1. Villages A and B
2. The distance is 50 km

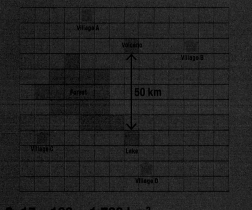

3. 17 x 100 = 1,700 km²
4. 100 x 5,000 = 500,000 trees
5. 1,700 x 5,000 = 8,500,000 trees

16-17 Melting mountain ice

1. 43,740 ÷ 9 = 4,860 litres per day
2. 43,740 ÷ 90 = 486 litres per day
3. 486 ÷ 60 = 8.1 litres per day
4. 486 ÷ 2 = 243 litres per day
5. 243 ÷ 3 = 81 litres per day

18-19 Feeling colder

1. The temperature difference between 3°C and -11°C is 14°C
2. The thermometer goes down to -20°C. 20 – 15 = 5, so there are 5 more degrees shown below -15°C.
3. The highest temperature was 4°C
4. The lowest temperature was -8°C
5. The temperature range from 4°C to -8°C is 12°C

20-21 Monsoon time

1. 8.5 cm
2. 6 + 8.5 + 7 = 21.5 cm
3.

4. Monday:
Tuesday:
Wednesday:
Thursday:
Friday:
Saturday:
Sunday:

22-23 Snowed in!

1. 2°C
2. 11th
3. 5°C
4. Monday
5. 4 + 2 + 3 + 1 = 10
6. 10 + 3 = 13

24-25 Deep-sea diving

1. Cone
2. Cuboid
3. Coral B
4. 4 + 4 + 3 + 5 = 16 sides
5. D – it is a pentagon

26-27 Global time

1. 3 pm – 7 hours = 8 am
2. 17:30 – 16 hours = 01:30
3. 8,000 ÷ 800 = 10 hours
4. 6 am (time at start) + 10 hours (length of flight – 8 (time difference) = 8 am
5. Depart: 06:00, Arrive: 08:00

MATHS GLOSSARY

ANALOGUE
An analogue clock has a round face with numbers and hands to point out the time.

AREA
The amount of two-dimensional space covered by a shape or object. For example, the area of a rectangle is calculated by multiplying the length of one of the short sides by the length of one of the long sides.

BAR CHARTS
A type of chart that uses vertical bars to show the frequency of different pieces of data.

CUBE
A three-dimensional shape that is formed from six square sides.

DECIMAL
Dividing whole numbers into smaller units. One can be divided into ten decimals (tenths), and these can be divided into ten smaller decimals (hundredths), and so on.

DIGITAL
A digital clock only uses numbers to tell the time.

DIVISION
Breaking up a number into smaller parts or seeing how many times one number will go into another one.

ESTIMATE
To produce an answer that is roughly equivalent to the correct answer. Estimating usually involves rounding up or down the numbers involved.

LINE PLOTS
Line plots show the size of different sets of data, using an 'x' or some other symbol to show the frequency or size of each data set.

NEGATIVE NUMBER
A number that is less than zero.

NUMBER LINE
A line that is divided into numbers and can be used to show a progression in increasing or decreasing values.

PICTOGRAM
A chart that uses small images to represent numbers and information.

PIE CHART
A type of chart that divides a circle into 'slices' according the proportion shown by each value. The bigger the value, the larger the slice on the pie chart.

PLANE SHAPE
A two-dimensional shape, such as a triangle or a square.

POPULATION
The number of people who live in a particular area, such as a town, region or country.

POSITIVE NUMBER
A number that is greater than zero.

PRISM
A three-dimensional shape that has two identical ends and flat sides. The shape of the ends determines the name of the prism, such as a triangular prism.

PYRAMID

A three-dimensional shape whose sides are formed from triangles that meet at a point above a base. The base can be a triangle, square, rectangle or any shape with three or more sides.

RECTANGLE
A four-sided shape where two sides are longer than the other two and all four corners have an angle of 90°.

RIGHT ANGLE
An angle of 90°.

ROMAN NUMERALS
A system of counting used by the Romans which featured combinations of letters instead of numbers.

1	I
5	V
10	X
50	L

SCALE
A number that shows how much a map or drawing has been made smaller. For example, a scale of 1:1,000, means that the image is 1,000 times smaller than the original, so 1 cm on the drawing represents 1,000 cm, or 10 m, in real life.

SOLID SHAPES
A three-dimensional shape, such as a cube or a sphere.

TABLE
A way of laying out numbers and information in rows and columns.

TALLY
A method of recording events or objects where a simple line is used to record each occurrence. Every fifth line is drawn across the previous four, creating easy-to-spot groups of five.

TRIANGLE
A shape with three sides. There are three types of triangle. An equilateral triangle has all three sides and angles the same. An isosceles has two of its sides and angles the same. A scalene triangle has all three sides and angles that are different.

VOLUME
The amount of space an object takes up. It is measured in cubic units, such as cubic centimetres (cm^3) or cubic metres (m^3).

INDEX

32

WEBSITES

www.mathisfun.com
A huge website packed full of explanations, examples, games, puzzles, activities, worksheets and teacher resources for all age levels.

www.bbc.co.uk/bitesize
The revision section of the BBC website, it contains tips and easy-to-follow instructions on all subjects, including maths, as well as games and activities.

www.mathplayground.com
An action-packed website with maths games, mathematical word problems, worksheets, puzzles and videos.

ACKNOWLEDGEMENTS

Published in paperback in 2015 by Wayland
Copyright © Wayland 2015
All rights reserved.

Dewey Number: 510-dc23
ISBN: 9780750289177
Ebook ISBN: 9780750285537

10 9 8 7 6 5 4 3 2 1

Wayland
An imprint of Hachette Children's Group
Part of Hodder & Stoughton
Carmelite House, 50 Victoria Embankment
London EC4Y 0DZ

Commissioning editor: Debbie Foy

Produced by Tall Tree Ltd
Editors: Jon Richards
Designer: Ed Simkins
Consultant: Steve Winney

Printed in China
An Hachette UK Company
www.hachette.co.uk
www.hachettechildrens.co.uk

The website addresses (URLs) included in this book were valid at the time of going to press. However, it is possible that contents or addresses may have changed since the publication of this book. No responsibility for any such changes can be accepted by either the author or the Publisher.

Picture credits
5t Shutterstock.com/Pavel Ilyukhin,
7t Shutterstock.com/Burben,
9t Shutterstock.com/Michael C. Gray,
9b all Shutterstock.com/CataVic,
11t and c Shutterstock.com/banderlog,
12cl both Shutterstock.com/
JungleOutThere, 15t Shutterstock.com/
Ammit Jack, 18-19 snowflakes
Shutterstock.com/Yulia Glam,
24t Shutterstock.com/Rostislav Ageev,
26c Shutterstock.com/Canoneer